Today Trading

Jackson Brooks

Jackson Brooks

Jackson Brooks

Copyright Page

Index

5:00 AM - The Mind Before the Market

At 5:00 AM a professional trader's day begins, and this first moment is crucial for what comes next. Before even thinking about charts, numbers, or news, it is essential to prepare the mind. Waking up early not only offers more time, but it allows a trader to take control of their morning without the chaos of the market that is yet to open. This is the ideal time to create a space of calm, stepping away from the screens for a while and immersing yourself in a routine that refreshes both the body and the mind.

Many traders start their day with meditation or breathing exercises. These practices, although simple, help clear the mind of unnecessary worries or thoughts. Deep, controlled breathing allows you to enter a state of calm, which is essential for making decisions under pressure later. By being silent, without distractions, you can visualize the day clearly. The best traders understand that their performance does not depend only on market movements, but also on the ability to maintain a focused and stress-free mind.

Physical exercise is also a fundamental part of many traders' routine. Running, yoga or simply a walk in the fresh air can make all the difference. Moving the body activates hormones such as endorphins, which improve mood and concentration. In addition, exercise prepares the body for long hours in front of the screen, helping to avoid physical fatigue. An active body contributes to an alert mind, which is essential when the market starts to move quickly. Each trader has their own way of exercising, but the goal is always the same: to feel good physically and mentally before starting the work day.

Another aspect that many traders integrate into their routine is personal reflection. This is a time to review goals, both short and long term. Thinking about the "why" behind each action is crucial. What drives you to continue on this path? What are the achievements you seek on a personal and professional level? These questions help you maintain a clear direction and avoid the feeling of simply reacting to the market. Clarity in goals allows you to make better and more focused decisions during the day.

It's not all about exercise and meditation. Some traders prefer to start their day with some light reading or listening to a motivational podcast. The goal is always to feed the mind with something positive. Avoiding social media or market news early in the morning can be key to not burdening the mind with unnecessary noise early on. This time is valuable and should be spent creating a mental environment in which calm and focus prevail.

The 5:00 AM routine is an investment in yourself. It's the time to be in control, to take charge of the day before the market dictates the pace. The best traders know that their performance is not measured just by how many hours they spend staring at charts, but also by how they prepare their mind to face those charts. A trader who starts the day with a clear, focused mind is in a better position to make quick, accurate decisions. This early hour is the foundation upon which the rest of the day is built. Without a prepared mind, the chaos of the market can easily overwhelm anyone.

In short, 5:00 AM is not about work, but about preparing to work well. It is the time a trader dedicates to himself in order to be able to perform at his best when the market opens. Without this mental and physical preparation, the following hours can become a constant battle against stress and emotions.

6:00 AM - Planning is Key

At 6:00 AM, one of the most important tasks for a trader begins: planning the day. After preparing the mind and body in the early hours of the morning, it is time to focus energy on understanding what is happening in the world and how it can affect the market. A successful trader does not trade on impulse, but with a well-thought-out plan. This is where detailed preparation becomes the key to seizing opportunities and avoiding unpleasant surprises.

The first thing to do at this time is to check global news. Markets do not operate in isolation; any event, from an important political decision to a change in the price of oil, can alter the course of financial markets. That is why professional traders spend time reading and analyzing what is happening in different parts of the world. Whether it is the opening of Asian markets, decisions by central banks or geopolitical tensions, everything can impact their operations. This early analysis allows them to anticipate possible movements and adjust strategies before local markets open.

In addition to global news, the economic calendar is another crucial aspect. This calendar includes key reports such as employment figures, inflation data, or statements from economic leaders. Traders who know this data in advance can avoid trading during times of high volatility or, if they are more risky, can take advantage of these movements to seek large profits. Knowing what important events are scheduled for the day allows the trader to be better prepared to deal with fluctuations that may arise.

6:00 AM is also the perfect time to review the previous day's positions. A disciplined trader evaluates what worked and what didn't, learning from both the wins and losses. This analysis allows you to adjust strategies as needed. It's not just about looking at the numbers, but understanding the "why" behind each outcome. Was there any unforeseen news that affected the market? Were emotional decisions made instead of following the plan? This constant review improves the ability to make smarter decisions in the future.

After reviewing what happened the previous day and keeping up with the news of the day, it is time to define the key levels for today's market. Professional traders identify support and resistance levels, points where the price of a stock or currency is most likely to change direction. This technical analysis helps predict possible movements and decide when to enter or exit a trade. Charts are drawn, alarms are set, and important levels are noted to be monitored during the day.

Although it seems like a technical process, planning also involves an emotional component. At this point, a trader asks himself how he feels. Are he anxious to make big trades or are he calm and focused? It is important to be aware of emotions before the market opens, as impulsive decisions often lead to costly mistakes. Planning involves not only numbers and charts, but also emotional preparation to face whatever comes during the day.

Discipline is key at this stage. Traders who wing it or enter the market without a clear plan often lose money. Having a well-defined strategy allows them to know exactly what they are looking for and what conditions must be met before opening a trade. The temptation to jump into a trade because it "looks good" can be strong, but without prior planning, it is easy to fall into traps that the market presents.

Finally, planning includes setting realistic goals. At 6:00 AM, the trader asks himself: What do I want to achieve today? It's not just about money, but about improving every day as a professional. Maybe the goal is to be more patient, to trade with less risk, or to follow market signals better. These goals allow you to stay focused and grow, both in skills and confidence.

In short, at 6:00 AM the real work of the trader begins. It is not about entering the market yet, but rather preparing for when the time is right. Planning is everything. Without solid preparation, it is easy to get lost in the volatility of the day. A successful trader spends this time reviewing, analyzing, and preparing his strategy, ensuring that when the market opens, he will be ready to make clear decisions based on his planning. This is the time to lay the groundwork for a productive and controlled day.

7:00 AM - Nutritious Breakfast and Positive Mindset

At 7:00 AM comes a crucial moment in the routine of any professional trader: breakfast. Although at first glance it may seem like just another activity of the day, the truth is that what is consumed in this first meal directly influences mental and physical performance during the following hours, when the market begins to move intensely. It is not just a question of eating to have energy, but of doing so strategically, selecting foods that promote concentration, focus and emotional stability.

A trader's breakfast should not be something heavy or loaded with processed sugars that only give a temporary energy boost and then cause a crash. The best traders opt for foods that release energy steadily throughout the day. A popular combination is to include proteins such as eggs or Greek yogurt, which help keep the brain alert, along with complex carbohydrates such as oatmeal or whole grain toast, which provide a long-lasting source of energy. It is also common to add healthy fats such as avocado or nuts, which are great for the brain, improving memory and the ability to make decisions under pressure.

Fresh fruits like blueberries, strawberries, or bananas are also great allies for a trader. Not only do they provide vitamins and antioxidants, but they also help keep blood sugar levels stable. This is crucial, as sudden spikes and drops in sugar levels can affect mood and mental clarity – just what a trader wants to avoid during key market hours. By eating a balanced diet, a trader ensures that their body is functioning at its full potential and that their mind is ready to react to any unexpected changes in the market.

However, breakfast is not just about food. 7:00 AM, while enjoying this meal, is also an ideal time to cultivate a positive mindset. After planning the day and analyzing market movements, this is the perfect time to reflect on personal and professional goals. Many traders use this time to practice gratitude, remembering the things they are grateful for in their life, which helps them maintain a positive outlook, even on the most difficult days. Having an optimistic mindset not only improves trading performance, but also helps you better deal with the stress and pressures of everyday life.

Some traders combine breakfast with listening to something inspiring. Whether it's a personal development podcast, a motivational talk, or just relaxing music, the important thing is to create a setting that's conducive to starting the day in the best possible mood. The mind is fed just like the body, and what you consume in the morning, in terms of information and emotions, can influence how you face challenges later on.

Moreover, it is at this time that many traders realize the importance of maintaining a steady pace, not only at work, but also in their personal lives. Eating slowly, enjoying each bite and taking time to think about the day ahead, is one way to avoid falling into the hectic and stressful routine that the trading world can often bring. The most successful traders understand that, although market hours can be hectic, they control how they start their day and what mindset they will bring to work.

This is also a good time to remind yourself of the importance of work-life balance. While eating breakfast, many traders reflect on how they are going to manage their time so that they don't neglect other areas of their life. They might ask themselves questions like: How can I make sure that, in addition to meeting my financial goals, I also take time for myself, my family, or my hobbies? These small morning reflections help create a broader sense of purpose and prevent the trader from getting lost in the frenzy of the market.

In short, at 7:00 AM, breakfast is not just a time to fill your stomach. It is an opportunity to prepare both your body and mind for what is to come. By choosing nutritious foods and pairing the meal with positive thoughts and a focused mindset, the trader ensures that he is in the best condition to face a day full of challenges. Eating well and thinking well at this key hour is not only a matter of physical health, but also of mental health. A calm and well-fed mind is better prepared to make clear and effective decisions when the market is moving quickly. This morning moment is a reminder that success in trading is not based solely on technical skills, but also on taking care of your body and emotional balance.

8:00 AM – Technical Review and Preparation of the Environment

At 8:00 AM, the time comes when the professional trader sits down in front of his screens and dives into the technical review of the market. This is a crucial step in his routine, as this is where the specific strategies that will be applied during the day are determined. After having reviewed the news and made an initial plan, it is now time to focus on the details, on the charts, the technical tools and on preparing the work environment so that it is ready when the market opens.

The first thing a trader does at this time is to open their trading platforms and check the charts of the assets they are following. Whether it is stocks, currencies or cryptocurrencies, it is essential to have a clear idea of how prices are moving. This is where Japanese candlesticks, trend indicators and support and resistance lines come into play. A trader does not jump into trading without first analyzing these technical levels well, as these points give them an idea of where the market may move and help them define possible entries and exits. The tools that the trader uses at this stage are essential for making informed decisions later.

In addition to charts, traders also use various technical indicators to reinforce their analysis. Some of the most common ones are moving averages, relative strength index (RSI), and MACD, among others. These indicators help identify whether the market is overbought or oversold, whether it is trending or in a consolidation period, and offer signals for potential trades. Every trader has their own set of tools that they prefer to use, and at this time of day, they set them up to make sure that everything is ready for when critical moments come. It is not just about knowing which indicators to use, but also knowing when to ignore them if market conditions change.

Another important aspect of 8:00 AM is preparing the work environment. A successful trader knows that organization is key to staying focused and avoiding mistakes. It is essential to have a clean and tidy space, with everything you need within reach: from a notebook to jot down ideas and strategies, to a bottle of water to stay hydrated. Sometimes, something as simple as having several well-organized screens can make the difference between missing an opportunity or making the most of it. Speed is essential in trading, and having everything well set up and ready to use helps avoid distractions and save time at key moments.

Also, at this stage, price alarms and alerts are set. The trader defines the levels at which he wants to be notified if the price reaches certain points, either to enter or exit a trade. This allows him to maintain control even when he is not looking directly at the chart. Alarms are an invaluable tool for traders who follow several assets at once, as they allow them to focus on what is important without getting lost in the multitude of information that the market constantly generates. Setting these 8:00 AM alerts correctly ensures that the trader does not have to be glued to the screen every second, but can instead concentrate on what really matters at any given moment.

This is also the time to check out expert reports or analysis, if the trader follows a trusted analyst. Some traders prefer to do all their analysis themselves, but others combine their own work with expert insights. Reading reports on the assets being followed can bring fresh perspectives and confirm or question what has already been seen on the charts. However, an experienced trader knows that while outside opinions can be helpful, the final decision should always be based on their own analysis and trading plan.

Another key aspect of this hour is scenario creation. A trader not only plans what he or she will do if the market goes up, but also what he or she will do if it goes down or if it stays in a sideways range. This is the time to think about the "what ifs." For example, if the price breaks a key resistance level, how will he or she react? What if, instead, it falls below an important support? Having a clear plan for each scenario prevents making impulsive decisions when the market starts to move. A prepared trader is not surprised by market movements, but already has in mind what he or she will do in any eventuality.

Finally, at 8:00 AM pending orders are also reviewed. These are trades that the trader has set to be executed automatically if the price reaches a certain level, without the need for manual intervention. Pending orders are a great way to ensure that opportunities are not missed while the trader is busy with other things or simply not in front of the screen. Reviewing them at this time allows strategies to be adjusted if technical analysis indicates that any changes are needed.

In short, technical review and environment preparation at 8:00 AM is critical to a trader's success. This is the time when the foundation on which the day will be traded is set. A professional trader leaves nothing to chance. From analyzing charts to setting up the workspace, every detail counts. This thorough preparation ensures that when the market starts to move, the trader is ready to act quickly, confidently, and accurately. This is the time to adjust tools, hone strategy, and make sure everything is in place for an efficient and focused trading day.

9:00 AM - Market Opening

At 9:00 AM, one of the most anticipated moments of the day for a trader arrives: the market opening. It is the moment when the calm that has accompanied the early hours of the morning transforms into a mix of excitement and extreme concentration. Everything that has been done up to this point, from planning to technical review, makes sense at this moment. The market opening marks the beginning of real action, where opportunities arise quickly and decisions must be made with precision.

When the market opens, the first thing that happens is a sudden increase in volatility. Prices start to move rapidly due to the accumulation of orders that have been placed overnight or since early morning. This is a critical moment, because many traders look to take advantage of the initial market movements to enter early positions and profit from sharp price changes. However, not all movements are reliable. A professional trader knows that while the opening can offer great opportunities, it is also dangerous territory if you are not prepared.

When the market opens, the trader's attention is drawn to the assets he has been monitoring. This is the time to observe how the support and resistance levels he has previously identified are behaving. Is the price breaking through a key level or is it bouncing back within the expected ranges? This is where patience comes into play. It is not about jumping into a trade right away, but rather about waiting for the right moment. Traders who are successful at the market open are not those who trade impulsively, but those who watch closely and react when conditions are favorable.

Another important aspect of this moment is that emotions can start to play a strong role. The adrenaline of seeing the charts move quickly can lead some traders to feel anxious about not missing out on an opportunity. However, more experienced traders know that emotions can be their worst enemy in these circumstances. Staying calm and clear-headed is key to making the right decisions. This means sticking to the plan that has been prepared in advance and not being carried away by the fear of missing out on a move or by the greed of wanting to take advantage of every fluctuation in the market.

The market opening is also a good time to adjust strategies according to current conditions. Sometimes, prices do not behave as expected during the technical review of the first few hours. In such cases, a trader has to be flexible and willing to make changes. It may be necessary to adjust entry or exit levels, or even discard some trades if the market shows signs that the risk is too high. Adapting to what the market presents is a skill that is developed with time and experience, and the opening is one of those moments when this skill is put to the test.

At the same time, it is at the opening that many traders activate their pending orders. These are trades that have already been set up to be executed automatically if the price reaches a certain level. For example, if the price breaks a resistance level that had been identified, the buy order is triggered without the trader having to intervene manually. This makes it possible to capture important movements, especially at such a dynamic moment as the opening, when prices can move quickly and reaction time is limited. Pending orders are a valuable tool for taking advantage of the market's speed without missing opportunities.

Communication also plays an important role at this time. Many traders are part of groups or communities where they exchange ideas and analysis in real time. The market opening is a time when these discussions become intense. Some traders share their observations on how certain assets are reacting or what movements are occurring in international markets. While it is important to remain independent in decisions, being in contact with other traders can offer additional perspective and confirm or question what is being seen on the charts. However, it is always crucial to remember that the final decision should be based on personal analysis.

Another important detail in this phase of the day is that not all openings are created equal. Sometimes the opening can be relatively calm, with limited movement, while other times it can be extremely volatile. A professional trader understands this and knows when it is better to be aggressive and when it is better to wait. It is not uncommon for the market to sometimes make misleading moves in the first few minutes, only to stabilise later. That is why more experienced traders often wait for the volatility to settle down before making important decisions, letting the market "show its hand" before taking action.

Finally, the market open is a test of a trader's preparedness. At 9:00 AM, all the previous hours of planning and analysis come into play. The trader already has a clear idea of what he is looking for, has defined his key levels, and is prepared both mentally and technically for whatever comes next. This is the time to execute the plan, to trust in the preparation, and to react to what the market presents. The open is not about guessing where the market is going, but about observing carefully, applying the planned strategies, and maintaining discipline in the face of the emotion of the moment.

In short, 9:00 AM marks the beginning of the action. It is the time when preparation and patience are combined with the ability to make quick decisions. The opening of the market is exciting, but also challenging, and only those who manage to stay focused and disciplined will be able to make the most of the opportunities it offers. This is the time when a trader puts everything he has worked on during the morning to the test and begins to execute his strategy with confidence and precision.

10:00 AM - First Operations

At 10:00 AM, it is time for the trader to start making his first trades of the day. After having spent the first few hours watching the market, analyzing charts, and fine-tuning strategies, it is time to put everything into action. The first trades are key, as they set the tone for the rest of the day. At this point, the trader has been monitoring the market movements since the open, patiently waiting for the right moment to enter a trade.

The first thing to understand is that the first trades of the day are usually not impulsive. While the excitement of seeing prices move can make it tempting to jump into a trade quickly, a professional trader knows that decisions must be based on careful analysis. This is where all the work of the previous hours is put to the test. Support and resistance levels have been identified, price alerts have been set, and a clear strategy is in place. Now, the trader watches closely to see if the market offers the conditions necessary to execute his plan.

At 10:00 AM, most experienced traders look to trade when the signals they have been waiting for are given. It could be that price is touching a key support level, or perhaps a breakout of a major resistance is occurring. This is the moment when the trading strategy becomes reality. But just because it is the first trade of the day does not mean you should rush it. A good trader does not feel pressure to enter a trade just for the sake of it. If the right conditions are not present, it is better to wait. It is not about trading for the sake of trading, but about trading smart.

Another important point is that first trades are often charged with emotion, especially if the trader is just starting out in this world. Adrenaline and anxiety can be factors that influence how the decision to enter the market is made. However, professional traders learn to manage these emotions. They understand that a trade should not be based on the emotion of the moment, but on solid analysis. Staying calm is crucial, as impulsive decisions can lead to unnecessary losses. Therefore, before making the first trade, it is important to take a moment to breathe, review the plan once again, and make sure that the decision is based on data and not impulse.

At this time, the trader also assesses the risk before making his first trade. No matter how attractive an opportunity may seem, the risks involved should always be considered. A good trader never risks more than he is willing to lose on a single trade. This means that before he clicks the buy or sell button, he is already clear about how much he is willing to lose if the market does not behave as he expected. For an experienced trader, risk management is a fundamental part of his daily routine. It is not just about seeking profits, but about protecting his capital and preventing a bad decision from having a devastating impact.

Early trades are also an excellent opportunity to assess whether the strategy is working as expected. Sometimes the market may behave differently than anticipated, and a trader must be flexible to adjust their plan if necessary. For example, if market volatility is greater than expected, it might be prudent to reduce position sizes to limit risk. Or, conversely, if the market is calm and stable, it may be time to increase trade sizes to maximize opportunities. The key is to be adaptable and not stick rigidly to a plan if market conditions change.

Once the first trade has been made, the trader's job is not over. This is where active trade management comes into play. This means that even though the trader has already entered the market, the trader is still keeping a close eye on how the price is behaving. If the trade is going in their favour, they can decide to let it run to maximise profits, or they can adjust the stop loss to lock in the profits made so far. If, on the other hand, the trade is going against them, the trader must be prepared to cut losses quickly and prevent a small loss from turning into a catastrophe. The ability to make quick and accurate decisions once in the market is what distinguishes successful traders from those struggling to stay afloat.

Around 10:00 AM, many traders also start to assess how the market is reacting compared to the economic news that was released earlier in the morning. Sometimes, early trades can be influenced by important economic data, such as employment reports or interest rate decisions. If any of these news items affect the market in an unexpected way, the trader has to adjust his strategies accordingly. This is where the ability to react quickly and adapt to new market conditions plays a key role.

The first few trades of the day also serve as a kind of "warm-up" for the trader. Even though he has already spent hours analyzing and preparing his strategy, entering the first trades of the day puts him right into the rhythm of the market. It is like an athlete who, after warming up, finally starts the match. These first trades help him tune in to the market, better understand how prices are moving, and confirm or adjust expectations that were held at the beginning of the day. With each trade, the trader is fine-tuning his approach, adjusting his mindset, and aligning himself with the market dynamics.

In short, at 10:00 AM, the trader starts executing the first trades of the day, but he does not do so impulsively. Each trade is carefully planned, based on technical analysis and risk management. Emotions are under control and decisions are made with clarity and precision. Although the market open has already passed, the first trades are crucial in setting the tone for the day. This is the moment when all the previous work is put into practice and where a trader demonstrates his ability to stay focused, disciplined and committed to his strategy.

11:00 AM - Reflection and Adjustment

At 11:00 AM, the trader enters a crucial phase of his day: reflection and adjustment. After having made some early trades and having observed the market behavior during the first few hours, it is time to pause for a while, analyze what has happened and, if necessary, adjust strategies. This is a fundamental part of a professional trader's daily routine. Although at first glance it may seem that trading is only about making quick decisions, constant reflection and adjustment are essential to improve performance and minimize errors.

The first thing a trader does in this hour is to review the trades he has executed. This does not necessarily mean that he has already closed all his positions, but it does involve making an assessment of how they are going. If trades are in progress, they are reviewed to make sure that everything is going as planned. Is the market moving in the expected direction? Have some of the objectives been achieved or are there any changes that need to be made? This is the time to confirm that the decisions made in the first few hours were correct or, failing that, to correct course if something is not working as expected.

Reflection is not just about seeing whether trades are generating profits or losses, but about analyzing the process behind each decision. The trader reviews whether his technical analysis was correct, whether the identified support and resistance levels have held, and whether the entry signals were clear. It is important not to fall into the trap of thinking that just because a trade is going well, the entire analysis was perfect. Sometimes, market movements can favor a trader even if he did not make the best decisions. Therefore, constant reflection helps to identify whether the strategies are well-founded or if there was simply a stroke of luck.

In case trades are not going as expected, this is the opportunity to adjust the strategy. It may be that the market has suddenly changed direction, or that economic news has had a bigger impact than expected. In these cases, a professional trader does not get stuck in his initial plan. The ability to adapt is essential in trading. If a trade has started to move against you, it is time to review the stop loss levels or even consider closing the trade to limit losses. If, on the other hand, the market is offering new opportunities that had not been considered before, this is the time to evaluate them and make the necessary adjustments.

Another important part of reflection at this time is emotional review. Trading can be emotionally intense, and sometimes emotions can cloud a trader's judgment. That's why it's crucial to pause at 11:00 AM to assess your mental state. Is the trader making decisions based on analysis, or is he or she reacting out of fear or greed? Discipline is a critical part of trading success, and this reflection helps keep that discipline in check. If the trader feels like he or she has been making impulsive decisions, now is the time to recalibrate and refocus on his or her plan.

In addition, in this phase the trader also reviews the general market conditions. The landscape may have changed since the opening, and it is important to be aware of any new trends or events that may be influencing prices.

Sometimes, the market may enter a consolidation phase, where prices stabilise and there are no major movements. In these cases, it may be necessary to adjust expectations for the rest of the day. If the market becomes more volatile than expected, the trader must be prepared to change his approach. The key is not to stick to a single plan, but to be flexible enough to adapt to what the market presents at any given time.

Part of this fine-tuning process also includes checking whether the price alerts you had set up are still valid. As the day progresses, support and resistance levels can shift, and it's important to adjust your alarms to reflect these changes. Maybe the price has broken through an important level and a new alert needs to be placed to track the next move. Or maybe the market has started to move in a tighter range, which might require adjustments to entries and exits. The goal here is to stay aligned with the market, making small adjustments that improve overall performance.

The 11:00 AM reflection is also a good time to review risk management. If the first few trades of the day have been successful, the trader may decide to increase their position size a bit to take advantage of the momentum. However, if previous trades have not gone as expected, it may be prudent to reduce risk on subsequent trades. There is no one-size-fits-all approach that works in all situations, so each trader must constantly assess how much they are willing to risk and adjust their exposure based on how the day is going. The goal is to protect capital, ensuring that a series of bad decisions does not compromise the overall account balance.

Additionally, at 11:00 AM the trader can take the opportunity to review any important news that may be coming out during the day. Some economic or political events have specific times, and it is crucial to be aware of them. For example, if an important economic report is expected to be released at noon, the trader may decide to avoid trading at that time due to the volatility it may cause. Planning for these events is part of daily reflection and helps minimize unnecessary risks.

In short, 11:00 AM is a time of reflection and adjustment in a trader's routine. It is the time to analyze how trading has gone so far, review strategy, adjust positions, and most importantly, maintain emotional control. The key to success in trading is not only making good decisions, but also learning from the decisions made and being flexible enough to change course when necessary. Constant reflection, coupled with the ability to adjust, allows a trader to improve day by day and adapt to ever-changing market conditions.

51

12:00 PM - Lunch Break

At 12:00 PM, a key moment arrives in the routine of any professional trader: the lunch break. Although it may seem like a trivial part of the day, taking a proper break is essential to maintaining focus and mental clarity for the rest of the day. For a trader, who spends hours in front of screens, analyzing charts and making critical decisions, this moment is not only necessary to recharge physical energy, but also to clear the mind and avoid emotional exhaustion.

By lunchtime, the market has usually gone through its most active phase of the morning. Some trades have been executed, an assessment has been made of how the day is going, and now it is time to take a step back. A common mistake that many traders, especially beginners, make is wanting to trade non-stop, thinking that every minute spent not looking at the charts is a lost opportunity. However, more experienced traders know that resting is just as important as trading, because a tired mind makes bad decisions. Hence the importance of taking a break at this time of day.

A good lunch for a trader should not only be nutritious, but should also help maintain a clear mind. Eating heavy or unhealthy foods can lead to drowsiness or a drop in energy levels, which will affect performance in the hours afterward. That's why many traders opt for light, balanced meals, such as salads, lean proteins, and foods that provide sustained energy without making them feel too full or sluggish. Food plays a big role in mental and physical state, so choosing wisely what you eat during this break can make a big difference.

But lunch isn't just about eating. It's also a chance to disconnect from the market and give your brain a break. During the morning, a trader has been exposed to a high dose of stimuli: rapid price changes, buy and sell decisions, constant chart analysis, and in some cases, even dealing with the stress of trades that don't go as expected. That's why it's vital to take advantage of this time to relax and disconnect, even if just for a little while. Some traders use this time to go for a walk, listen to music, or do an activity that allows them to distract themselves and recharge their energy.

The lunch break is also an ideal time to reflect on how the first half of the day has gone. While more technical review has already been done in the previous hours, this time allows for a calmer perspective. How have trades gone? Have any good decisions been made? How is the market in general? This type of reflection is less formal than that done in front of screens, and is often more productive, as it occurs in a relaxed environment, away from the pressure of the market. Sometimes, by taking a break, ideas become clearer and errors or possible improvements that were not seen before can be identified.

Another important aspect of a lunch break is that it helps a trader avoid mental exhaustion. Trading is an activity that demands a lot of concentration and energy. Every decision has a direct impact on the results, and staying focused for long hours without a break can lead to exhaustion, which increases the chances of making mistakes. Taking a break allows the mind to refresh, so that when the trader returns to the screens, he or she will be ready to make decisions clearly and without the fatigue that can build up after several hours of continuous work.

Also, during lunchtime, the market tends to calm down a bit. It is not uncommon for volatility to subside, especially in some markets, making this a good time to step away without fear of missing out on great opportunities. Many experienced traders prefer not to trade during these quieter hours, as market movements tend to be less predictable. They use this time to recharge and come back stronger for the afternoon sessions, which often bring a new wave of activity.

The lunch break also provides an opportunity to adjust the approach for the rest of the day. After having reflected on the morning's trades and having disconnected for a while, the trader can re-plan his next actions. Sometimes, market conditions have changed during the morning, or the news that was expected has not had the expected impact. This moment of pause is ideal to re-evaluate the trading plan and decide if adjustments to the strategy are necessary. It may be that the trader decides to adopt a more conservative approach if the day has not been favorable, or that he decides to increase his exposure if he has had success in the first few trades.

Some traders also use lunchtime to catch up on market news or read up on topics that interest them. While disconnection is important, so is staying informed. During this time, many check out economic headlines, global news, or events that could influence the markets in the following hours. It's a way to stay up-to-date without being directly involved in trading. However, it's important not to be tempted to overload yourself with information. The goal of the break is to relax, not to fill yourself with more stress, so any activity done during this time should be balanced and not add unnecessary pressure.

In short, the lunch break is much more than just a time to eat. It is a fundamental part of a professional trader's routine, as it allows him to recharge his batteries, disconnect from the market and reflect on how the first part of the day has gone. A trader who does not take the time to rest can suffer the consequences of mental and physical exhaustion, which negatively affects his performance in the following hours. By using this break properly, the trader can come back with a clear mind, a fine-tuned strategy and the energy needed to face the second half of the day with confidence and precision.

1:00 PM – Personal Development

At 1:00 PM, a professional trader's daily routine shifts away from the trading screens to focus on something equally important: personal development. This is a crucial time in the day, because while trading success depends on technical skills and knowledge of the markets, personal growth is what really helps a trader stay focused, disciplined, and resilient in the face of challenges. It's not just about being a better trader, it's about being a better version of yourself. And that takes time and dedication.

Personal development can take many forms. For some traders, this is the time to read books that inspire them or teach them new skills. These books don't have to be directly related to trading. In fact, many successful traders find value in reading about psychology, leadership, business, or even philosophy. These reads help to expand the mind, see the world differently, and adopt new ways of thinking. Reading about topics outside of trading can also offer valuable lessons that apply indirectly to decision-making in the markets. For example, a book on leadership could teach how to better manage emotions under pressure, a crucial skill for any trader.

Another common form of personal development is practicing meditation or mindfulness. While it may sound out of the ordinary for the trading world, many professionals have found that these practices help them stay calm and mentally clear, even on the most chaotic of days. Meditation teaches you to focus on the present, clear your mind of distractions, and manage stress more effectively. Some traders dedicate this hour to guided meditation sessions or simply to being silent, allowing their thoughts to flow and calm down. This allows them to return to the market with a more focused mind and a greater ability to make rational decisions.

Physical exercise also plays an important role in personal development. Some traders take advantage of this time to exercise, whether it is a quick routine at home or a visit to the gym. Keeping the body moving not only improves physical health, but also releases endorphins, which improve mood and concentration. For a trader, being physically active is vital, as spending so many hours sitting in front of a computer can be exhausting for the body. A regular exercise routine helps keep the body and mind in balance, which in turn improves the ability to make clear and quick decisions throughout the rest of the day.

Another aspect of personal development to consider is continuous learning. The world is constantly changing, and trading is no exception. During this time, a trader can enroll in online courses, participate in webinars, or watch educational videos on topics that interest them or that they want to master. Education doesn't have to be limited to trading alone; learning about business management, marketing, or even technological skills can open up new opportunities in the future. Devoting time to intellectual growth is an investment that will always pay off in the long run.

In addition to the more tangible aspects of personal development, 1:00 PM is also a great time to set goals. Many traders spend this time reviewing their long- and short-term goals. What do they want to accomplish in the next few months, both in their trading career and in their personal life? Setting clear goals allows them to stay focused and motivated. It's not just about making more money or doing better in the market; it can also be something as simple as learning a new skill, improving a personal relationship, or adopting healthier habits. Taking a moment to visualize the future and map out a plan to get there is a great form of personal development.

Personal development isn't just about improving technical or physical skills; it also encompasses emotional well-being. Some traders use this time to reflect on their emotions, evaluate how they've been feeling throughout the day, and work on their emotional intelligence. Trading can be an emotional roller coaster, with highs and lows that can be difficult to handle. Understanding how emotions affect decisions is key for any successful trader. Practicing self-awareness and self-reflection is an essential part of this process. A trader who is aware of their emotions is less likely to make impulsive mistakes and more able to make rational decisions under pressure.

Another important aspect of personal development is socialising. Spending so many hours alone in front of screens can be isolating, so it's crucial to maintain relationships with friends, family or colleagues. Some traders use this time to get in touch with their support network, whether it's by texting, calling a friend or even participating in trading communities. Talking to other people helps to release tension, share experiences and remember that life isn't all about trading. Healthy relationships outside of work are key to maintaining a work-life balance.

Finally, this time for personal development can also be used to simply rest and recharge. Sometimes the best personal growth comes from doing nothing, from allowing yourself a moment of pause in the middle of a busy day. Traders who allow themselves to rest, even for just a few minutes, return to work with renewed energy and a clearer mind. This rest is necessary to avoid burnout, which can lead to poor decisions or, worse, long-term health problems.

In short, 1:00 PM is the perfect time to focus on personal development within a professional trader's routine. Whether through reading, meditation, exercise, or reflection, this time allows you to grow as an individual and better prepare yourself to face the challenges that lie ahead, both in the market and in life. Personal development not only improves trading performance, but also brings balance, well-being, and satisfaction in other areas of life. Dedicating this hour to yourself is an investment in long-term success, because at the end of the day, a trader can only perform at their best if they also feel good about themselves.

2:00 PM - Market Review

At 2:00 PM, the professional trader turns his focus back to the market to do a thorough review of how the day has progressed so far. This is a crucial part of the daily routine, because the market has been in motion for several hours, and reviewing trades and overall conditions is essential to making informed decisions and adjusting the strategy if necessary.

The purpose of the market review at this time is twofold. On the one hand, the trader needs to assess how open positions have evolved since the morning. You may have entered into some trades at the opening or in the early hours of the day, and now is the time to see how they are developing. Have stocks or assets moved in the expected direction? Have unexpected events occurred that have affected prices? Reviewing open positions allows the trader to assess whether they need to be held, adjusted or even closed. This decision is based on technical and fundamental analysis, but also on the trader's ability to quickly adapt to changing market conditions.

In addition to reviewing individual trades, it is important to analyze the overall behavior of the market. During the morning, the market may have shown a clear trend, either bullish or bearish, but as the day progresses, conditions may change. Trends may begin to weaken, support or resistance levels may have been broken, or even a new trend may have appeared. At 2:00 PM, the trader has to be very attentive to these changes. This is where flexibility becomes a key tool. Sometimes, maintaining too rigid a stance on a strategy can lead to unnecessary losses. This is the time to evaluate whether the initial strategy is still valid or whether it needs to be adjusted.

Technical review also plays an important role in this phase of the day. Many traders use charts with technical indicators such as moving averages, RSI, Bollinger bands, and others to analyze market behavior. At 2:00 PM, it is a good opportunity to revisit those charts with fresh eyes. In the morning, the market may have been very volatile, but at this point in the day, trends may have started to stabilize or give clearer signals. By reviewing the charts again, the trader can confirm whether the signals he observed in the morning are still valid or whether there are new patterns that suggest a change in price direction.

Another important aspect of market review is the assessment of news and events. Throughout the day, economic or political news may have emerged that impacts the markets. This is a good time to catch up on any relevant announcements that have occurred since the morning. For example, if a key economic report has been released or if a major company announcement has been made, this news can have an immediate impact on asset prices. The trader must be able to integrate this information into his analysis and adjust accordingly. In some cases, the news may confirm a trend he had already identified, while in others it may generate unexpected moves that require a re-evaluation of his trades.

Market review also includes risk management. As trades develop, the trader may need to adjust his or her stop-loss levels or take profits based on market movements. By 2:00 PM, trading may have progressed far enough that it is prudent to lock in some profits, especially if market conditions begin to become more uncertain. This is where the trader's ability to effectively manage risk comes into play. Knowing when to adjust a stop-loss to protect a profit or when to close a position that is not performing as expected is crucial to keeping the account healthy and avoiding large losses.

At this time of day, some traders also take the opportunity to identify new opportunities in the market. Although they may already have trades open from the morning, market conditions may have changed, opening new doors to enter additional trades. Reviewing at this time can show emerging patterns that were not present before, and this gives the trader the opportunity to capitalize on those moves. However, it is important not to fall into the trap of trading for the sake of trading. Each new opportunity should be backed up by solid analysis and should fit within the trader's overall strategy.

As the evening progresses, trading volume in some markets may begin to slow down, meaning price movements may be slower or more predictable. However, in other markets, activity may increase, especially if there is an event scheduled for later or if international markets are expected to influence prices. In any case, the trader must be prepared to adapt to these changes. While it is tempting to relax after a day of intense trading, this is a key time to stay alert and continue with a detailed review of the market.

Market review at this time is also a good opportunity to learn. A professional trader is always looking for ways to improve. By analyzing past trades and how the market has behaved, it is possible to identify patterns or mistakes that can be avoided in the future. Every trading day offers lessons, and this time of review is ideal to reflect on what has worked and what has not. Even if the day has been successful, there is always something that can be improved, whether in terms of analysis, risk management or the execution of trades. A trader who does not take the time to learn from his experiences is destined to repeat the same mistakes.

Furthermore, market review doesn't have to be a solitary process. Many traders choose to join communities or discussion groups where they can share ideas and analysis with other professionals. At this time of day, it's common for some traders to exchange opinions on how they've seen the market or comment on important news that has affected prices. Participating in these types of discussions not only offers new perspectives, but can also help validate or question decisions that have been made so far. Collaboration and knowledge sharing are valuable tools for any trader who wants to continue improving.

In short, the 2:00 PM market review is a fundamental step in the daily routine of a professional trader. This is the time to evaluate how open positions have evolved, adjust the strategy as necessary, and keep an eye on any changes in market conditions. It is a process that requires concentration, analysis, and above all, the ability to quickly adapt to whatever the market throws at you. By keeping a constant and detailed review of the market, the trader ensures that he is always one step ahead, prepared to face any challenges that may arise, and ready to take advantage of any opportunities that may present themselves in the rest of the day.

3:00 PM - Keeping Calm in the Final Hours of the Market

At 3:00 PM, in the final hours of the market, a professional trader knows that it is crucial to remain calm. These final hours are often a roller coaster of emotions, as market movements can be unpredictable and often more volatile. However, rather than getting carried away by the emotion or pressure of the moment, the experienced trader understands that the key to ending the day successfully is to stay focused, make decisions with a cool head, and avoid the temptation to make impulsive moves.

As the market closes, it's common for some traders to try to take advantage of the day's final moves, either to make one last trade or to close out open positions. At this time, market volatility can increase, especially if there's a major event coming up, such as an earnings report or some major economic news. But this is where the importance of discipline comes into play. While it may seem tempting to take advantage of those quick moves, the risk of making a mistake by acting hastily is high. Instead of getting carried away by the frenetic market action, a professional trader carefully evaluates whether it's worth entering a trade or whether it's better to watch and wait.

Staying calm in these final hours also means being aware of one's emotional state. After a full day of trading, it's natural to feel fatigued, stressed, or even excited if things have gone well. These feelings can cloud judgment and lead to impulsive decisions. For example, if the market has gone against a trader's positions during the day, frustration can lead them to try to "make up" their losses by making last-minute trades without proper analysis. This is known as "revenge trading," and it's one of the most dangerous traps a trader can fall into. That's why, at 3:00 PM, it's vital for a trader to pause, take a deep breath, and ask themselves whether the decisions they're making are based on logic or emotion.

Another important aspect of staying calm in the late hours of the market is risk management. As the day draws to a close, it is time to re-evaluate open positions and make decisions based on risk analysis. If there are trades that have been profitable, it may be prudent to take profits before the market closes, thereby avoiding possible sharp price swings in the final minutes. On the other hand, if a trade has not worked out as expected, it may be time to close it and take the loss, rather than leaving it open in the hope that the situation will improve in the evening or the next day. Professional traders know that you cannot control the market, but you can control how you manage risk. This mindset allows them to make more objective decisions and protect their capital.

Emotional control is only one part of the equation. Technical preparation also plays a big role in the final hours of the market. A trader who has followed his plan since the morning, checking the market, adjusting strategies, and managing his trades, will arrive at 3:00 PM with greater mental clarity. He knows exactly what condition his portfolio is in and what he needs to do in the next few hours. So part of staying calm at this point is having done the prep work so there are no last-minute surprises. Preparation reduces stress and allows the trader to act more rationally and less impulsively.

In many cases, the last few hours of the market do not offer clear opportunities, and this is where patience and calm are essential. An experienced trader knows that it is not necessary to trade every minute of the day to be profitable. Sometimes, the smartest thing to do is to simply observe the market without making unnecessary moves. In fact, some of the most successful traders spend the last few hours of the day simply reviewing their trades, evaluating their performance, and planning for the next day, rather than looking for new opportunities. This attitude is the result of years of experience and understanding that trading is not just about making money at every moment, but about maintaining consistency over the long term.

For other traders, these final hours can be a time of reflection. Reviewing what has happened during the day, both in terms of personal performance and market behavior, can offer valuable lessons. A trader who remains calm at the end of the day can take a moment to analyze which strategies worked and which didn't, what emotions arose during trading, and how he or she handled stress. This self-assessment not only helps improve technical skills, but also allows for emotional growth, strengthening the trader's ability to better manage emotions on future trading days.

Staying calm in the final hours also means keeping an eye on the moves of the big market players. As the market closes, it is common for institutions and investment funds to make adjustments to their positions. This can cause significant price movements in certain assets, which may seem attractive to more inexperienced traders. However, professional traders understand that these movements are often out of their control and that trying to follow them can be dangerous. Instead of chasing these moves, they prefer to stay true to their strategy, watching the market cautiously and avoiding acting impulsively.

One of the biggest benefits of staying calm in these final hours is that it allows the trader to end the day with a sense of control and satisfaction. A trader who has managed their day well, followed their plan, and remained calm under pressure can close out their day knowing they have done their best, regardless of the results. This mindset is essential for long-term sustainability in trading, as success is not measured by daily gains alone, but by the ability to remain disciplined and focused day in and day out.

In the end, trading is a marathon, not a sprint. The final hours of the market are yet another test of a trader's ability to handle pressure and make informed decisions. Staying calm in the moment is what separates successful traders from those who act on impulse. A professional trader understands that the market will always offer new opportunities, and that it is more important to preserve capital and discipline than to try to win at all costs at every moment. By staying calm, a trader ensures that he is in a strong position to face the next day, ready to continue building on his long-term success.

4:00 PM - Market Close

At 4:00 PM, one of the most important moments in the routine of any professional trader arrives: the market closes. This moment marks the end of a day that has been full of analysis, decisions and emotion management. Although the market closes, a trader's work does not end here, as the market close represents an opportunity to reflect, evaluate and prepare for the next day.

The first step during market closing is to review all open positions. A professional trader makes sure to close those that do not make sense to hold overnight, as markets can experience unexpected movements outside of regular hours. Some assets can be affected by breaking news or movements in international markets that are still open. Therefore, one of the key aspects of closing is to decide whether it is prudent to keep any open positions or whether it is better to liquidate them to avoid unnecessary risks. This is a time of evaluation, where the trader compares the performance of his trades with his expectations and makes adjustments if necessary.

After making sure that positions are under control, the trader conducts a deeper analysis of the day. This is the time to review in detail each trade that was made. Why was a specific decision made? Was it based on sound analysis or was there an emotional component that played a role? This is often an exercise in constructive self-criticism. Successful traders know that each day offers valuable lessons, and the market close is the ideal opportunity to absorb those lessons. By analyzing both winning and losing trades, the trader can identify patterns of success and areas where improvement is needed.

This post-market analysis not only focuses on individual trades, but also on the overall strategy that was implemented during the day. In some cases, a trader may realize that the strategy worked perfectly, while in others he or she may identify weak points. The close of the market allows for adjustments to be made to improve performance on future days. For example, if a strategy that is normally effective did not work on this occasion, the trader can investigate whether there were any external factors that influenced it or whether it was simply a bad day. This reflection is key to developing a mindset of continuous improvement.

In addition to evaluating his own performance, a trader also looks at the overall market behavior. How did the major indices perform? Were there any relevant events that moved the market significantly? This evaluation not only allows the trader to better understand the dynamics of the day, but also helps him prepare for the next day. In many cases, the market close offers clues about what might happen tomorrow. For example, if the market closed at a key support or resistance level, this can indicate that significant moves are expected the next day. That's why professional traders always keep an eye on closes, not only for what it means for the present, but for what it can reveal about the future.

Another important aspect of market closing is risk management. While trading involves taking risks, a professional trader always makes sure that those risks are under control. During the closing, it is common to review whether the position sizes were appropriate in relation to the total capital. If at some point during the day more risk was taken than planned, the market close is the time to reflect on why that decision was made and how to avoid it in the future. This methodical approach allows the trader to stay within the limits of his trading plan, protecting his capital in the long term.

The market close also offers an emotional respite. After a busy day, a trader has the opportunity to relax a bit and process the emotions that arose during the day. Even the most experienced traders feel the pressure of the market at some point, and the close allows them to let go of that tension. Some traders use this moment to take a short break, disconnect from their screens, and regain energy before preparing for post-market analysis. This pause is important to maintain emotional balance and avoid mental exhaustion, especially after intense days.

Even though the market has closed, professional traders know that the work is never really done.

Part of the routine after the close is to begin planning for the next day. This includes reviewing scheduled economic news, upcoming earnings reports, and any other events that may influence the market. By being prepared in advance, traders can start the next day with a clear idea of what to watch for and what opportunities might arise. Preparation is key in trading, and the market close is the perfect time to lay the groundwork for a new day.

The close of the market is also a good time to analyze the overall performance of the portfolio. While day trading focuses on individual trades, a professional trader always has the bigger picture in mind. How has the portfolio performed over the past few weeks or months? Are financial goals being met? This broader analysis allows the trader to make adjustments to their long-term strategy if necessary, and ensure that they are moving steadily toward their goals.

Additionally, the market close provides an opportunity for continued education. Many successful traders spend time after the close reading books, articles, or analyzing historical charts to improve their skills. The market is constantly changing, and a trader who doesn't continue to learn is left behind. Whether it's learning new strategies or delving deeper into the analysis of economic events, the time after the close can be very productive if used for personal and professional growth. Traders who commit to learning something new every day have a better chance of staying competitive in the market over the long term.

In short, the market close is a time for reflection, evaluation, and preparation. It is not just the end of a trading day, but an opportunity to learn from the day's experiences, adjust strategy, and plan for the future. A trader who approaches the close with calm and discipline is better prepared to face the challenges of the market in the days to come. Although the market officially closes at 4:00 PM, the work of a professional trader continues, with the goal of continuing to improve and grow in his or her career.

5:00 PM - Work-Life Balance

By 5:00 PM, a professional trader's workday may have come to an end, but there's one crucial aspect that many overlook: work-life balance. In the world of trading, where emotions are always running high and snap decisions can have a significant impact on results, it's easy to fall into the trap of letting work consume every moment of the day. However, successful traders understand that to stay on top of their game, they must find a healthy balance between their career and personal life.

Trading is a mentally exhausting activity. From the moment the day begins, the trader is immersed in charts, analysis, and financial decisions that require a high level of concentration. After hours of being in that constant state of alert, time is necessary to disconnect, relax, and recharge. This disconnection is not only important for mental health, but also improves performance at work. A trader who does not take time to rest runs the risk of burnout, which can lead to impulsive and costly decisions in the markets. At 5:00 PM, the trader must close the screens, put aside market analysis, and dedicate time to activities that take him away from the financial world.

Work-life balance is not just about getting some rest, but also about nurturing personal relationships. Trading is a solitary career in many ways. While some traders work in teams, most spend most of their time in their own minds, making individual decisions. That's why it's critical to take time after the market closes to connect with friends, family, or loved ones. Sharing a family dinner, going for a walk with a friend, or just having a nice conversation can make a big difference in how you cope with the stress of work. These interactions provide a sense of well-being that helps maintain a balanced perspective. A trader who feels connected to their personal environment is more emotionally resilient and can better handle market pressures.

In addition to relationships, physical well-being is another aspect that should not be neglected. Sitting in front of a screen all day can cause the body to suffer. Lack of movement, coupled with constant stress, can create tension in the body that affects not only physical health, but also mental health. It is common for traders to experience pain in the back, neck, or hands after hours of being in the same position. Therefore, at 5:00 PM, it is the perfect time to exercise or participate in some physical activity that helps release the stress accumulated during the day. Whether it is a session at the gym, a yoga class, or simply a walk in the fresh air, physical exercise not only improves health, but also clears the mind and helps release the tensions of the day.

Another key component of work-life balance is time for personal development. Often, in the quest to be better at work, it is forgotten that personal growth is just as important. Spending time on hobbies, learning new skills, or simply reading a good book are all ways a trader can nurture their personal side, moving away from a sole focus on the market. This personal growth is essential, as it provides a sense of satisfaction and fulfillment that goes beyond financial success. At the end of the day, being a good trader is important, but being a balanced and fulfilled person is critical to having a satisfying life in the long run.

Maintaining a routine outside of work that includes time for relaxation, exercise, and personal development is not only beneficial for mental and physical health, but it also improves performance at work. A trader who has a balance between his personal and professional life has more mental clarity and is able to make more objective and less impulsive decisions. Trading is a field that demands that you always be at 100%, and the best way to ensure that level of performance is to take care of yourself outside of work hours. In the end, a trader who feels good about himself and his surroundings is a trader who can face the challenges of the market with greater confidence and serenity.

It is important to remember that work-life balance is not something that is achieved overnight. It requires effort, discipline, and above all, an awareness of the importance of this balance. Some days work may seem more demanding, and at other times personal life may require more attention. The key is to find a middle ground where both areas nourish each other. A trader who finds this balance understands that his life is not defined only by his success in the markets, but also by the quality of his relationships, his physical and mental well-being, and his ability to enjoy moments outside of work.

For many traders, one of the biggest challenges is "turning off" after work hours. The nature of the market, with its constant movements and ever-present opportunities, can cause a trader's mind to always be thinking about the next trade, even after the market has closed. However, a disciplined trader learns to set boundaries. Part of work-life balance is knowing when to completely disconnect from the market. This can mean avoiding checking financial news, stopping thinking about trading strategies for the next day, and focusing on activities that provide respite. Some traders even establish a specific routine to help their minds switch off, such as practicing meditation or dedicating time to a creative activity.

Finally, work-life balance is also about finding satisfaction in both aspects. It's not about working just to have free time, or disconnecting just to be more productive. A trader who achieves this balance enjoys both his work and his personal life. He sees work as a valuable part of his day, but doesn't let it consume all of his time or energy. Likewise, he values his personal life as a sacred space that provides him with happiness, fulfillment, and the rest necessary to continue performing at his best in his work.

In conclusion, at 5:00 PM, when the market closes and the work day is over, it is time to focus on work-life balance. Making time for personal relationships, body care, personal development, and mental disconnection is essential for any trader looking to not only be successful in the markets, but also lead a full and balanced life. Balance is not just a strategy to be a better trader, it is a strategy to be a more well-rounded person. And ultimately, that balance is what allows a trader to stay in the game for the long haul, without burning out or losing passion for what they do.

6:00 PM - Preparation for the Next Day

At 6:00 PM, a trader's day is not quite over yet. Even though the market has already closed, the next crucial step is preparation for the next day. This is a routine that may seem tedious to some, but professional traders understand that success in the markets is not just based on what you do during trading hours, but also on what you do after the market closes. Proper preparation is what separates a trader who simply goes with the flow of the market from one who is ready to take advantage of every opportunity. It is at this time that the trader lays the groundwork for the next trading day, allowing him to face the market with confidence and clarity.

The first step in preparation is to review the economic calendar for the next day. Employment reports, interest rate decisions, company earnings announcements, and other economic events can have a significant impact on the markets. Knowing these events in advance is essential to avoid surprises and plan accordingly. A trader who does not pay attention to this data can get caught in a trade at the wrong time, losing money on an event that could have easily been anticipated. Therefore, reviewing the economic calendar is not only part of preparation, but also part of risk management. Knowing when these events are expected allows the trader to adjust their strategies or even decide whether or not to trade that day.

In addition to reviewing the calendar, another important aspect of preparation is technical analysis. This is where the trader returns to the charts, but this time without the pressure of making immediate decisions. It is time to analyze market movements from a calmer and more objective perspective. Support and resistance levels, current trends, and possible pattern formations that could indicate a change in direction or a continuation of the trend are reviewed. This is a fundamental part of the process, as it allows the trader to identify opportunities before they present themselves. Instead of reacting to market movements, the trader who prepares properly can anticipate them and be ready to act when the right moment comes.

Technical analysis also includes reviewing open positions and adjusting pending orders. A disciplined trader does not leave these decisions to the last minute during market hours, when pressure is at its highest. Instead, he uses this preparation time to adjust his stop loss or take profit orders, based on recent market performance. This allows him to better manage risk and protect his capital. Additionally, some traders prefer to place limit orders for the next day, ensuring that if the market hits a key level while they are not in front of the screen, their trade will be executed automatically. This is an effective way to ensure that you do not miss opportunities while maintaining a disciplined strategy.

Another crucial aspect of preparing for the next day is reviewing recent news and news that could impact the markets. Even if a trader has already reviewed the economic calendar, unscheduled news can also impact trading. This includes political events, changes in monetary policies, or unexpected news such as natural disasters or international crises. Being aware of these events allows a trader to adjust his or her expectations and, if necessary, modify his or her strategy for the next day. Preparation is not only about anticipating what can be predicted, but also being ready for the unexpected.

At this stage, many traders also take the opportunity to review their trading journal. This journal is an essential tool for long-term growth. In it, the trader records all of his or her trades, along with the reasons behind each one and the results obtained. Reviewing the journal not only helps to learn from mistakes, but also to identify patterns of success. By reviewing the day's trades, the trader can see whether he or she followed his or her plan correctly or whether he or she allowed emotions to influence his or her decisions. This process of self-assessment is key to continuous improvement and is a fundamental part of the routine of any trader seeking long-term success.

Preparation also involves adjusting your mindset for the day ahead. Trading is not just about technical analysis or news. Mindset is an integral part of success in this field. As the end of the day approaches, the trader must begin to visualize the day ahead, not only from a technical standpoint, but also emotionally. What challenges might arise? How will you handle stress if things don't go as planned? This mental preparation is just as important as technical preparation, as a trader with a calm and focused mindset is better equipped to make rational decisions and avoid impulsive mistakes.

A less technical but equally important aspect of preparing for the next day is the organization of the workspace. A clean and tidy work environment may seem like a trivial thing, but it has a significant impact on productivity and concentration. At this point, the trader should make sure that his desk is clear, his trading tools are ready, and everything is in order for the next day. Having a well-organized workspace helps to start the day with a focused mindset and without distractions. Small details like these can make a big difference in a trader's effectiveness and ability to trade efficiently.

Finally, preparation for the next day also includes adequate rest. Although it may not seem like part of the job, getting a good night's sleep is essential for a trader. Decisions in the market require mental clarity, and that clarity can only be achieved when the brain is well rested. Lack of sleep impairs the ability to make quick and accurate decisions, which is essential in trading. A trader who is serious about his preparation understands that the day does not end when the market closes, but when he has laid the foundation for a good rest. Getting a good night's sleep is the last step in effective preparation, ensuring that the body and mind are ready to face the challenges of the next day.

In short, at 6:00 PM, preparation for the next day is an essential part of a professional trader's routine. From reviewing the economic calendar and news, to adjusting open positions and organizing the workspace, each step is designed to ensure that the trader is ready to face the market with confidence and clarity. Preparation not only involves being aware of what might happen, but also adjusting the mindset and environment to maximize performance. A trader who prepares properly is not only ready to take advantage of market opportunities, but also to handle challenges with calm and discipline.